THE ADVENTURES OF AWFUL KNAW

Designed for audiences of 7—11 year-olds, *The Adventures of Awful Knawful* was commissioned and staged by the Royal Shakespeare Company as their first Kids' Show for many years.

'For children from six to 96 who think they've seen everything, the RSC have come up with *Awful Knawful*, a truly coarse comic sci-fi panto . . . The plot goes something like this. The Voice, a frightful unseen figure, tries to control the world by SPONGGING (Awful language for brain-washing) the Greatest People on Earth. The Voice succeeds in SPONGGING the Greatest Memory Man and the Greatest Athlete; soon Awful Knawful aided by the Perfect Pet are the only survivors. Who is the Voice? How does the Perfect Pet survive her attack by tin-openers? How does Awful crawl over the minefield? Who will have to play the most Horrible Game of Doctors and Nurses? All will be revealed . . . '

Time Out

'Peter Flannery and Mick Ford have written a show which offers little or nothing to children who enjoy sentimental songs or crying their eyes out over Bambi or Snow White. But for the sort of tough, modern children who are supposed to spend all their time watching Starsky and Hutch and the like, it is sure-fire material.'

The Financial Times

Accompanying the playtext is the music written for the show by Mick Ford, as well as an introduction and production notes by Peter Flannery.

in the same series

RARE EARTH
a programme about pollution
devised by the Belgrade
Coventry Theatre in
Education Company for 9–
11 year-olds

SWEETIE PIE
a play about women in
society devised by the
Bolton Octagon Theatre in
Education Company
edited and introduced by
Eileen Murphy for 14 year-
olds upwards

OLD KING COLE
a play by Ken Campbell
originally written for the
Victoria Theatre, Stoke-on-
Trent for 8–12 year-olds

SKUNGPOOMERY
a play by Ken Campbell for
8–12 year-olds

TIMESNEEZE
a play by David Campton
originally written for the
Young Vic Theatre Company
for 7–11 year-olds

**THE INCREDIBLE
VANISHING!!!**
a play by Denise Coffey
originally written for the
Young Vic Theatre Company

PLAYSPACE
four plays for children by
contemporary writers
(**The Cutting of Marchan Wood**
by Richard M. Hughes;
The Boy without a Head
by Edward Lucie-Smith;
Tamburlane the Mad Hen
by Adrian Mitchell;
**The Legend of Scarface and
Blue Water** by Niki Marvin)
for 8–14 year-olds

SNAP OUT OF IT
a·programme about mental
illness devised by the Leeds
Playhouse Theatre in
Education Company edited
by Roger Chapman and
Brian Wilks
with an introduction by
Brian Wilks for 15 year-olds
upwards

PONGO PLAYS 1–6
six short plays by Henry
Livings for 12 year-olds
upwards

SIX MORE PONGO PLAYS
six short plays by Henry
Livings for 12 year-olds
upwards

**THEATRE-IN-EDUCATION
PROGRAMMES: INFANTS**
five programmes for 5–8 year-
olds edited by Pam Schweitzer

**THEATRE-IN-EDUCATION
PROGRAMMES: JUNIORS**
four programmes for 8–12
year-olds edited by Pam
Schweitzer

**THEATRE-IN-EDUCATION
PROGRAMMES: SECONDARY**
four programmes for 12 year-
olds upwards edited by Pam
Schweitzer

**THE ADVENTURES OF
GERVASE BECKET**
or The Man Who Changed
Places a play by Peter Terson
originally written for the
Victoria Theatre, Stoke-on-
Trent edited and introduced
by Peter Cheeseman for 8–14
year-olds

SCHOOL FOR CLOWNS
a play by F. K. Waechter
translated by Ken Campbell
for 7–15 year-olds

THE
ADVENTURES OF
AWFUL KNAWFUL

A Play by Peter Flannery
and Mick Ford

Introduced by Peter Flannery
With music by Mick Ford

Eyre Methuen · London

First published in Great Britain 1980
by Eyre Methuen Ltd
11 New Fetter Lane, London EC4P 4EE
The Adventures of Awful Knawful copyright ©1980
by Peter Flannery & Mick Ford
Introduction copyright ©1980 by Peter Flannery
Music copyright ©1980 by Mick Ford

ISBN 0 413 46630 2

Printed in Great Britain by
Whitstable Litho Ltd., Millstrood Road, Whitstable, Kent.

Introduction

THE ADVENTURES OF AWFUL KNAWFUL is a play intended
for eight to twelve-year-olds though it may also be enjoyed by
younger children and by parents. It was commissioned by the
Royal Shakespeare Company and was first performed by them at
the Warehouse, Covent Garden, in December/January 1978/9.
Obviously the RSC saw the play as a seasonal alternative to
traditional pantomime but *Awful Knawful* in fact has no
particular relevance to Christmas and can be presented at any
time of the year and in many different kinds of production. It is
the story of Awful Knawful, a fearless stuntman, who is
transported to a world of failures, nutcases, strange creatures and
megalomaniacs. This world is dominated by a disembodied Voice
whose plan to invade and rule Earth with an army of killer robots
is finally thwarted by Awful's extraordinary courage. Before he
finally tracks down the Voice however he has a series of
encounters with the various inhabitants: the Perfect Pet, Croton
the Zombie, P.C. McKnee, etc. They all have two things in
common. Firstly, they are all scared stiff of the Voice and,
secondly, they are all absolutely useless at everything they try to
do. And the Voice doesn't make it easy for Awful to find him.
Minefields, giant ants and a psychopathic choir are just some of
the dangers that cross his path.

In the RSC's production directors Howard Davies and John
Caird and designer Chris Dyer made great use of the Warehouse's
lighting and sound systems and its five entrances and exits. The
action of the play all took place on one set, the adventure playground, to which portable scenery or props, like doors or
trolleys, were sometimes added for specific scenes. The adventure
playground consisted largely of boxes and see-saws but the stage
was dominated by a large frame from which ropes and hooks
were hung. Characters could swing from these, climb up them to
hide, or use the whole apparatus as a prop of some kind, e.g.
Professor Madchat's Perfect Mousetrap. It is perfectly possible
though to stage the play much more simply, without any major
construction on stage and without sophisticated lighting effects.
Certain sound effects, either recorded or reproduced live, are
essential, as are certain props. But both can be kept simple. The
same is true of most of the costumes.

For anyone contemplating a production of the play in, say, a
school hall or a studio there are notes at the end of the text
which might help. There is also a score of the live music which
accompanied the RSC production as well as some ideas about
how this might be used in other productions.

Peter Flannery

The Adventures of Awful Knawful was first presented at the
Warehouse, London on 20 December 1978 with the following
cast:

AWFUL KNAWFUL, *the bravest man on earth*	Richard Derrington
PROFESSOR MADCHAT, *a nutcase*	Nigel Terry
GERONIMO, *an animal invented by the Professor*	Charlotte Cornwell
JAKOPO & MARLA, *two stupid killers*	Rory Edwards & Michele Copsey
DR. KNOTINISHANKI, *the greatest memory man on earth*	Kenneth McClellan
LASSE FEVER, *the fastest runner on earth*	Charles Wegner
CROTON, *a zombie*	Nicholas Le Prevost
P.C. McKNEE, *the greatest policeman on earth*	Kenneth McClellan
DR. BLOOD, *the greatest surgeon on earth*	Mike Hall
FLORENCE, *his nurse*	Colin McCormack
THE KILLER ROBOT, *another of the Professor's inventions*	Mike Hall
JASPER & DENIS, *the perfect children*	Colin McCormack & Charles Wegner
AN ARMY OF KILLER ANTS	Themselves
A GIANT SPIDER	Colin McCormack
THE KID, *a gunslinging desperado*	Kenneth McClellan
THE SHERIFF, *his deadly enemy*	Mike Hall
A MOUSE	A Mouse
A CHOIR OF MAD KILLERS	A Choir of Mad Killers
THE MASTER, *a maniac*	Iain Mitchell/Peter Clough
MUSIC, *by the greatest musicians on Earth*	Jeremy Barlow, Peter Cameron, Nigel Garvey, Brian Newman, Peter Whittaker

Directors: John Caird & Howard Davies
Designer: Chris Dyer
Assistant to the Designer: Gilly Hebden
Lighting: Brian Wigney & Eddie J. Freed
Sound: John A. Leonard

The performance area is an adventure playground containing boxes, planks, tyres and, where possible, ropes, swings and see-saws. There should be a bicycle somewhere and a banner saying 'AWFUL KNAWFUL IS COMING HERE TODAY'. Onstage and elsewhere the audience should see newsboards carrying the following headlines: 'TOP DOCTOR KIDNAP DRAMA'/ 'POLICE CHIEF VANISHES'/'OLYMPIC RUNNER MISSING'/ 'GREAT INVENTOR DISAPPEARS'/'AWFUL KNAWFUL TO MAKE DARING PUBLIC APPEARANCE'. A playleader and some helpers are on the set as the audience enters so that the kids can use the playground and/or ask questions about what's going on.

Scene One
The noise of a helicopter landing near the playground. Enter SID POWER *with some* BODYGUARDS. *They appear to be very nervous and straightaway begin to clear the playground of any kids.*

SID: Everybody sit down. Come on. Nothing's going to happen till you all sit down.

LEADER: Will everybody sit down, please.

SID: Come on. We can't have you all milling about. In fact — let's see all your hands. Come on — hands on heads. Awful stays in the helicopter till all the hands are on all the heads. Right (*To the* BODYGUARDS:) I don't like the look of those two. Check them over.
The BODYGUARDS *search members of the audience.*

LEADER: Mr. Power?

SID: Yeh?

LEADER: Mr. Power, I think we all realise the enormous courage it takes for Awful to make this public appearance . . .

SID: Dead right. Look at all these people who've gone missing.

LEADER: But the kids were wondering if they could see Awful in action. You know — do a stunt for us.

SID: Forget it. Listen, it's dangerous enough just for the boy to be out. There's no way he's going to do any stunts — OK?

LEADER: Yes, but we thought —

SID: Look, it's strictly a personal appearance — all right? And if there's any more aggravation that chopper goes straight back into the sky and Awful doesn't appear at all. OK?

LEADER: OK. Just thought I'd ask.

SID *takes one more look around the audience.*

SID (*to* BODYGUARDS): Let's get Awful.

Exeunt SID *and the* BODYGUARDS.

LEADER: Listen, we'll ask Awful ourselves when he arrives, eh?

SID *re-appears carrying a microphone. The* BODYGUARDS *hover nervously at the door.*

SID (*to the* BODYGUARDS): OK? Right. (*Drum roll.* SID *talks into the mike.*) Do not bat an eyelid. Do not even blink. He's on his way. Here. Today. In the flesh. At great personal risk. For you and you only. The bravest stuntman the world has ever known. The great, the fabulous, the unbelievable — put your hands together, please, let's hear your applause for the very one and only MISTER AWFUL KNAWFUL! Awful! Awful! Awful! Awful!

SID *and the* BODYGUARDS *lead the chant. Fanfare. Enter* AWFUL KNAWFUL. *Rousing music. He does a circuit of the stage, waving and occasionally trying to shake hands. But he is heavily screened by the* BODYGUARDS *who are determined to protect him. He goes to the centre of the stage. The music ends.*

SID: Ladies and gentlemen — Awful Knawful!

SID *and the* BODYGUARDS *lead more applause.*

OK. That's it. Let's go, Awful. Back to the chopper. Bye, everybody.

They usher AWFUL *towards the exit.*

LEADER: Mr. Knawful?

SID (*to the* PLAYLEADER): Look, I told you before —

AWFUL (*to the* BODYGUARDS): Will you lot get out of the way! (*to the* PLAYLEADER:) Yeh?

LEADER: Mr. Knawful, the kids and I were wondering if you'd mind doing —

SID: Look, Awful, we've got to get going —

AWFUL: Sid.

SID: Yes, Awful?

AWFUL: Shut up.

SID: Yes, Awful.

AWFUL: Well?

LEADER: We were wondering if you'd do a stunt for us.

AWFUL: What — here? Now?

LEADER: Just something simple — to show everybody how great you are.

AWFUL: Have you got a bike or something?

LEADER: Yeh.

SID: Don't do it, Awful. Something's bound to go wrong.

AWFUL: I'm fed up with all this marching about shaking hands, Sid. I want to do stunts again. I'll do it.

He starts looking closely at the lay-out of the playground.

SID (*to the* PLAYLEADER): I'll kill you if anything goes wrong.

AWFUL: I'm going to come up this ramp.

SID (*into the mike*): He's going to come up this ramp. No, Awful, don't do it.

AWFUL: I'm going to fly through the air.

SID: He's going to hurtle through space. Please, Awful. Don't do it!

AWFUL: I'm going to ditch the bike.

SID: He's going to ditch the bike. Awful, I'm begging you.

AWFUL: And land with a backward somersault . . . . . . there.

SID: And land with a double backward Kaligari somersault on this very spot. Ladies and gentlemen, you don't know how lucky you are here today. For you and you alone — Awful risks everything.

AWFUL *is riding the bike round the playground, examining the stunt.*

Awful. Are you ready?

AWFUL *nods and exits on the bike to start his run-up.*

Ladies and gentlemen, silence please as the death-defier begins his run-up. (*Drum roll.*) Here. He. Comes!

AWFUL *re-enters on the bike. As he reaches the top of the ramp the lights go out and strange loud noises fill the air. Silence.*

Scene Two

AWFUL *is unconscious on the ground. The bike has gone and so have* SID, *the* BODYGUARDS *and the* PLAYLEADER. *The* VOICE *arrives. His approach and arrival are always denoted by*

*the same music or sound effect. His departure is denoted by the
reverse effect. When he speaks the lights should flicker if possible.*

VOICE: This is The Master speaking. In exactly one minute it will
be Spongg Time.

The VOICE *goes.* AWFUL *begins to wake up, groggily.*

AWFUL: Eh? Did somebody say something? Where is everybody?

A long tube is thrown onstage. It has buttons and wires on it.
PROFESSOR MADCHAT *has thrown it and now he speaks to
someone or something offstage.*

PROF (*off*): Fetch! Fetch when I tell you to fetch! Go on! Pick
it up!

Bewildered, AWFUL *picks up the tube. Enter the* PET, *an
animal invented by the professor. It should look as if it was
put together by a lunatic. It has a voice but its words are
barely comprehensible, which is why its speeches appear in
brackets. They see each other.*

AWFUL: Who are you?

PET: (It's Awful Knawful! My hero!).

AWFUL: What?

Enter PROFESSOR MADCHAT, *eccentrically dressed.*

PROF: Ah there you are, you stupid pet! (*to* AWFUL): What are
you doing with that bone?

AWFUL: Well, I —

PROF: Are you a dog?

AWFUL: No, but —

PROF: Then put it back where you found it! (AWFUL *does so.*)
Now, you. When I invent a pet I expect it to be able to do a
simple thing like fetching a bone. Fetch! Look, it's easy. I'll
show you.

*He gets down on his hands and knees and picks up the tube in
his mouth. The* VOICE *arrives. The* PET *pushes* AWFUL *aside
and hides him.*

VOICE: Spongg Time!

PROF: Morning, Voice. Nice day.

VOICE: Don't call me 'Voice', Professor Madchat. Call me
'Master'.

PROF: Look here, Voice, I want to show you something.

VOICE: Not now, Professor — it's Spongg Time!

Fanfare. Enter JAKOPO *and* MARLA, *the* VOICE'S *servants.
They are joined together permanently. They lead on*
DOCTOR KNOTINISHANKI.

Ah, Jakopo and Marla — my faithful servants. Who have you

brought me for spongging today?

MARLA: Doctor Knotinishanki.

JAKOPO: The greatest memory man on Earth.

VOICE: Welcome, Doctor Knotinishanki, welcome to my kingdom. It's a great honour for you to meet me. Greatest memory on Earth, eh?

KNOT: That is correct.

VOICE: Very well then. Who played outside left in the Tottenham Hotspur team which won the double in 1961?

KNOT: Cliff Jones. The full team was Brown, Henry, Allen, Blanchflower —

VOICE: Most impressive, Doctor Knotinishanki. Marla, Jakopo. Spongg him.

The ritual spongging takes place. This might consist, for example, of stamping an indelible mark on the victim's forehead.

JAK/MAR: Spongg him. Spongg him. Ready — spongg. Steady — spongg. Go! Spongg!

KNOTINISHANKI *goes rigid and makes a strange noise.*

VOICE; Let's test this great memory of yours *now*, Doctor. What is the capital of England?

KNOT: Is it Paris?

VOICE: Very good. Perhaps you could tell me your name, Doctor Knotinishanki?

KNOT: Erm . . . could you repeat the question, please?

VOICE, JAKOPO *and* MARLA *laugh uproariously*.

VOICE: Congratulations, Doctor. You are now one of the most stupid people in my kingdom. Which is saying something. Take him away.

JAKOPO *and* MARLA *take the* DOCTOR *away*. VOICE *is jubilant*.

Oh, excellent! What a wonderful kingdom. Professor, do you realise there are only two more Earth people to spongg and then I will have wiped out all of their leaders? All their heroes and heroines. All their brilliant people will be gone and then I will be able to take over Earth with my robot army. Then everybody will be sponged. Especially the kids. Earth will be powerless. I will be ruler.

PROF: Then what?

VOICE: Then what what?

PROF: Then what are you going to do with the Earth when you've taken it over?

VOICE: Make it exactly like here, of course.

PROF: But, Voice, this place is a nightmare!

    JAKOPO *and* MARLA *bring on* LASSE FEVER. *He is in a crouched position.*

VOICE: Ah, another Earthman for spongging. Only two more left.

MARLA: Yes, master. This man: Lasse Fever — the fastest runner on Earth.

JAKOPO: And Awful Knawful — the bravest man on Earth.

VOICE: And then the Earth shall be mine. On with the spongging. Why is he crouching like that?

MARLA: Master, he was in this position when he was transported.

VOICE: Very well. Jakopo. Marla. Spongg him!

JAK/MAR: Spongg him. Spongg him. Ready — spongg. Steady — spongg. Go!

    On the word 'go' the Athlete runs off.

VOICE: You imbeciles! You let him escape! You must suffer for this!

JAK/MAR: Mercy, master!

VOICE: Very well. I'll give you a chance. Capture him within thirty seconds and I'll spare you.

PET: (one, two, three, four, etc.)

JAK/MAR: Yes, master. Thank you, master. The master is good. The master is good.

MARLA: This way!

JAKOPO: This way!

    They are pulling in opposite directions.

PET: (Nine, ten, eleven, etc.).

JAKOPO (*to the* PET): We'll get *you* later.

    Exeunt JAKOPO *and* MARLA, *running.*

VOICE: Cretins.

PROF: Voice, while we're waiting, could I show you this?

    He holds up the tube.

VOICE: Not another of your useless inventions?

PROF: It's for your robot army.

VOICE: Ah, yes, the robot army. Thanks to them the Earth shall soon be mine —

PROF: Yes, don't start all that again, Voice, please!

VOICE: They will conquer Earth.

PROF: Yes, I know — I invented them.

VOICE: Earth will crumble before the might of my robot army.

PROF (*exasperated*): Not without this!

VOICE: A bone?

PROF: This isn't a *bone*. This is the most crucial part of the robots. It's —
The ATHLETE *is chased across stage by* JAKOPO *and* MARLA.

VOICE: Jakopo. Marla.

JAK/MAR (*stopping*): Yes, Master?

VOICE: You only have twenty seconds left.

JAK/MAR: Thank you, master. The master is good. The master is good.
Exeunt JAKOPO *and* MARLA. VOICE *is laughing.*

PROF: Please, Voice, pay attention! Inside this tube is a homing device which I will attach to the chief robot. When the robots have conquered Earth the homing device will be turned on by remote control and all the robots will come back to you.

VOICE: And all because of that silly tube? Brilliant! Then I can use the robots again to conquer more worlds. Mars, Jupiter, Uranus.

PROF: Yes. When it's perfected, that is.

VOICE: You mean it doesn't work!

PROF: Of course it works — sometimes.

VOICE: Then go away and make it work all the time. And do it quickly. I want to launch my invasion in a day or two.

PROF: But, Voice, I need more time.

VOICE: You'd have plenty of time if you didn't waste it inventing stupid animals. Take your device and your ridiculous pet and get out of here, Professor!

PROF: I'd be delighted. Come on, Pet, we're leaving.
Exit PROFESSOR. *The* PET *stays. Enter* LASSE FEVER *pursued by* JAKOPO *and* MARLA.

VOICE: Ten seconds left. Nine, eight, seven, six, five, four, three, two, one, zero.
They capture him.

JAK/MAR: Got him, master.

VOICE: So, Mister Lasse Fever — you're the fastest runner on Earth, eh?

FEVER: That is so, yes.

VOICE: Marla, Jakopo. Spongg him.

JAK/MAR (*hanging on to him this time*): Spongg him. Spongg him. Ready — spongg. Steady — spongg. Go! Spongg!
They spongg him. He goes rigid and makes a noise.

VOICE: Let's see you run now, Fever.

FEVER *runs off very badly. They all laugh at him.*
What are you two laughing at?
JAK/MAR: Sorry, master.
VOICE: Bring on our final victim: Knawful — the bravest man on
   Earth. We'll see how brave he is when we've spongged him.
   Ha, ha, ha.
JAKOPO: Master, we can't find him anywhere.
VOICE: What?
MARLA: We haven't had time to look —
VOICE: You incompetent idiots. You must suffer for this. You
   know what I'm going to do, don't you?
JAK/MAR: Yes, master. Give us agony.
VOICE: Exactly. Agony. Take *that.*
   A horrible noise. JAKOPO *and* MARLA *writhe in agony for a
   few seconds. It stops.*
   Now get after him. Find him and bring him in for spongging.
JAK/MAR: Yes, master. Thank you, master. The master is good.
   The master is good.
   They go.
VOICE: Once Knawful is turned into a coward by the spongg
   nobody will be able to stop me from taking over the Earth.
   All power shall be mine!
   The VOICE *goes.*

Scene Three
AWFUL *emerges from behind the* PET.
AWFUL: They're after me — I've got to get out of here. I'm not
   staying here to get spongged. Wait a minute though. I'm the
   only one who can do anything about this now. It's up to me
   to save Earth.
PET: (Yes! My hero!).
AWFUL: But how? How am I going to do it? There must be a
   way.
PET (*tapping him on the shoulder*): (The homing device, Awful).
AWFUL: What? On, shut up, you, will you? I'm trying to figure
   this out. To save the Earth I've got to . . . . get to that Voice!
PET: (Yes!).
AWFUL: But how?
PET (*tapping him again*): (The homing device).
AWFUL: Look — shove off, will you? I've got to get to that

Voice and stop him. But how? The homing device!

PET: (Very clever!).

AWFUL: That tube thing. That'll lead me to him. But how can I get it?

PET: (Go and nick it from the Professor, Awful).

AWFUL: Push off, tin head. I'm trying to save Earth. If only I could find the homing device.

PET: (The Professor! The Professor!).

AWFUL: I know — the Professor!

PET (*clapping*): (Hooray! Very good!).

AWFUL: That's it! I've had enough of you! Now GET LOST!

PET (*going*): (That's not very nice, is it?)

AWFUL: I've got to find that Professor. But where do I start looking? This place is absolutely crazy!

The noise of a police-car approaching, sirens blaring.

What's that? It's the cops!

P.C. McKNEE rides straight across stage on a bike. The siren fades as he goes.

AWFUL: Oy! Cop! Have you seen the Professor? Hold on a minute, that was my bike! Oy!

He runs off after McKNEE, leaving his gloves on the ground.

Scene Four

Enter CROTON, a zombie. He is another of the professor's inventions. He moves slowly and emits low grunting noises instead of speech. He is very strong and very unpredictable. He sees the gloves and takes a fancy to them. He puts them on. Sirens. McKNEE rides on and dismounts.

McKNEE: Stealing gloves, eh, zombie? You're under arrest!

CROTON begins to throttle him.

All right!

CROTON releases him.

All right! You're *not* under arrest!

Exit CROTON.

And let that be a lesson to you! Next time I won't be so lenient! Zombies!

McKNEE gets on his bike and goes, accompanied by sirens.

Scene Five

Enter PROFESSOR MADCHAT heading for his laboratory.

PROF: Voice is completely power mad! Treating me like an imbecile! Where's that stupid pet got to?

The PET dashes in and sits up and begs.

Ah, there you are. What? You want the bone? Marvellous! You want me to throw it for you? Terrific! What a brilliant pet! (*He throws the bone. The PET picks it up in its teeth.*) Now bring it back to me. (*The PET runs off.*) Bring it back to me! You stupid animal! Come back!

The VOICE arrives.

VOICE: Professor! Have you perfected that homing device yet?

PROF: Not quite, Voice.

VOICE: Then get a move on! And don't whatever you do let it fall into the wrong hands. I don't want anybody tracking me down, do I?

PROF: Oh, absolutely not, Voice. Must dash.

VOICE: Goodbye, Professor.

The VOICE goes.

PROF: I must find that pet before it buries the homing device somewhere!

Exit the PROFESSOR.

Scene Six

Enter AWFUL.

AWFUL: Where is everybody? I've never seen a place like this. Everything's weird. It seems to be getting dark as well. (*It gets brighter.*) Stupid place. I don't think anything's normal round here.

(*Sirens. Enter McKNEE on his bike. He stops and dismounts.*)

At last. A normal human being. Excuse me, officer?

McKNEE: Yes, sir?

AWFUL: Look, you're never going to believe this but there's this Voice character and he's planning to take over Earth and –

McKNEE: You're under arrest!

AWFUL: What for?

McKNEE: Hearing things!

AWFUL: Hearing what things?

McKNEE: You're under arrest again!

AWFUL: What for now?

McKNEE: Asking questions!

AWFUL: What questions?

McKNEE *hits him with his truncheon*.

McKNEE: Don't get violent with me!

AWFUL: Who's getting violent?

McKNEE (*hitting him again*): Stop asking questions! You're new here, aren't you?

AWFUL: Yes, I was just doing this stunt and —

McKNEE: Right! I'll need full details!

He takes off his helmet and takes a notebook from inside it. There is a spongg on his forehead.

What are you looking at?

AWFUL: Nothing.

McKNEE: Name? Doesn't matter! Address? Doesn't matter! What were you before you came here?

AWFUL: I'm a stuntman.

McKNEE: Cor! You mean jumping off cliffs, swimming rivers, that sort of thing?

AWFUL: That's right. I'm Awful Knawful.

McKNEE (*hitting him*): Big head!

AWFUL: Don't keep doing that!

McKNEE: You looking for trouble? Where's your spongg? Doesn't matter! Got to dash. Somebody's robbing a bank over there.

AWFUL: Where? Quick. Let's get them. I'll give you a hand.

The cop is already heading off in the opposite direction. Sirens.

What sort of a copper are you? I give up. No, I can't give up. I'm the only one who hasn't been sponged. I've got to get that homing device. If only somebody would help me.

Enter the PET *with the homing device.*

Oh, no — not you again! (*It drops the device at his feet.*) Look, not now — can't you see I'm busy?

PET: (It's the homing device, Awful).

AWFUL: All right. I'll throw it in that river and you go and get it. And I hope you drown.

He makes to throw it.

PET: (No!).

He recognises it.

AWFUL: The homing device! What a stroke of luck!

PET: (Stroke of luck!).

AWFUL: Now all I've got to do is activate it. (*He tries.*) It doesn't work. Come on, you stupid thing. You're supposed to lead me to the Voice.

He struggles with it in vain. The PET takes it, presses some knobs, pulls some wires, bangs it on the floor, gives it back to him and presses one more button. It starts working.

AWFUL: I knew there had to be a simple answer!

PET: (Thanks a bunch!).

It starts to drag him round the stage. The VOICE is heard in the distance.

AWFUL: It's working! Come on! Take me to the Voice!

VOICE (*distant*): Aaaaaaargh! No! Knawful has the homing device and he hasn't been spongged! He must be stopped. I must not be tracked down.

AWFUL: It's homing in on him. Goodbye, thing.

PET: (Goodbye, Awful).

AWFUL: Here I go! Awful Knawful!

Exeunt PET and AWFUL in different directions.

Scene Seven

Enter JAKOPO and MARLA dragging DOCTOR KNOTINISHANKI.

KNOT: Please — let me go.

JAKOPO: Quiztime Doctor Knotinishanki! First question coming up.

MARLA: Five seconds to answer: what day comes after Tuesday?

JAK/MAR: Five, four, etc.

KNOT: I know it, I know it. It's . . . . . . wait!

JAKOPO: Time's up!

They laugh and whack him.

JAKOPO: Again, Marla.

MARLA: Second question. How many players in a five-a-side football team?

MAR/JAK: Five, four, etc.

KNOT: I know, I know . . . . . . wait!

JAK: Time's up!

They whack him again — but less enthusiastically.

JAKOPO: Get lost, Knotinishanki — we're bored with you!

KNOTINISHANKI *runs off. MARLA and JAKOPO turn on the audience.*

MARLA: Right. Now it's your turn.

JAKOPO: Five seconds to answer. What is the capital of Outer
    Mongolia?
JAK/MAR: Five, four, three, two, one. Time's up!
    They laugh and whack the audience.
MARLA: Now over here.
JAKOPO: Five seconds to answer. Who invented Scotland?
JAK/MAR: Five, four, three, two, —
    The VOICE *arrives quickly.*
VOICE: Marla! Jakopo!
JAK/MAR: Yes, wise one?
VOICE: See where your stupid bungling has got me! You and
    that crackpot Professor with his stupid homing device!
JAKOPO: But, master, we —
VOICE: Knawful has it. He must be stopped. He must be
    spongged. I must not be found.
MARLA: But, master, you're all-powerful. How can a human
    harm you even if he does find you?
VOICE: He must *not* find me!
JAKOPO: But, master —
VOICE: Don't keep arguing with me, you clods! Take *that!*
    They writhe in agony for a few seconds.
    Get after him. I'll lead him through the most dangerous parts
    of the kingdom. I'll send a ferocious wind to slow him up. But
    you must get him!
JAK/MAR: Yes, master. We obey. Get him. Get him. Which way?
    This way. No, this way, you fool. No, this way!
VOICE: *Get* him! *Get* him! *Get* him!
    Exeunt JAKOPO *and* MARLA *in confusion. The* VOICE *goes.*

Scene Eight
Enter AWFUL *being pulled by the device. He looks dishevelled.*
AWFUL: Voice! Voice! Stone the crows! I'm going round in
    circles. I've been up hills, across streams, through hedges, back
    up the same hills again, in and out of swamps — and I'm
    getting nowhere. I can't keep up with the Voice. He's always
    one step ahead of me. Why don't you stop and face me? Oh
    well, at least I'm still on the trail.
    The device stops working. He bashes it.
    Don't stop now. Not in the middle of nowhere — with
    those two killers on my tail. Come on. It's useless. (*He looks*

around). Where am I? What's that funny noise?
The sound of explosions, getting gradually louder.
Sounds like explosions. Can't be. Where am I?

VOICE (*distant*): You're in a minefield, Mr. Knawful.

AWFUL: What — ?

VOICE (*distant*): I said you're in a minefield.
The explosions are getting louder.

AWFUL: A minefield! It's a good job this thing stopped
working or else it might have —
It starts working. It drags him towards the VOICE.
Oh, no!

VOICE: Oh, yes! Come and get me.

AWFUL: It's started following him again! It's going to drag me
across the minefield. I'll get blown to bits if I touch the
ground!
*He crosses the stage by jumping and swinging from obstacle
to obstacle. Despite some near-misses he eventually arrives
safely.*
I did it!
Enter JAKOPO *and* MARLA.

JAKOPO: Let's get him, Marla!

MARLA: No, stupid. Why's he just standing there?

JAKOPO: Yeh. Why isn't he running away from us?

AWFUL: What's the matter? Too scared to come and get me?
Big cowards!

JAK/MAR: We're not cowards!

AWFUL: What's the matter then? Too stupid?

JAK/MAR: We're not cowards and we're not stupid!

AWFUL: Prove it.
They dash onto the minefield and get blown up.
So long, blockheads!
Exit AWFUL.

JAKOPO: I'm getting fed up with this. Why are we always
getting it?

MARLA: I thought the mighty one was supposed to be
helping us?

JAKOPO: Yeh! Where's that ferocious wind he promised us?
A ferocious wind blows them off stage.

JAK/MAR: Aaaaaaaaaaaaaaaargh!

Scene Nine
DOCTOR BLOOD *wheels a door onto the stage, struggling into the ferocious wind. He pushes it to the centre and steps through it. He closes the door behind him. The wind stops.*
DOCTOR: What a draught!
While the DOCTOR *is talking,* FLORENCE *his nurse enters with a trolley. On the trolley are a milk bottle, a length of tubing, a funnel, a mallet and a handsaw.*
DOCTOR: Next! I said 'next' ! Well? What are you waiting for? Must be something the matter with you or you wouldn't be here. Come on, I haven't got all day. I haven't had a patient for months — have I, Nurse?
NURSE: Just because you've had a few little accidents, Doc.
DOCTOR: Yeh. Anybody been sick today? Anybody got anything interesting?
NURSE: Anybody got anything disgusting? Come on. Diarrhoea?
DOCTOR: Green monkey disease? I can cure it.
NURSE: He can cure anything.
DOCTOR: I could cure it easy as standing on my head.
He points to his foot.
Look at that one, Nurse! You look terrible!
NURSE: Shocking! What's the matter with you? Nothing?
DOCTOR: Nothing? That's what you think. We'll soon find out. Just a minute till I put this telescope round my knee.
He puts a stethoscope round his neck and examines somebody.
You know your trouble, don't you? You're hollow. What about you over there?
He examines somebody's arm.
This leg'll have to come off! Just a minute! Nurse!
NURSE: Yes, Doc?
DOCTOR: I've got an amputation over here. I'll need some blood. Loads of it.
NURSE: Yes, Doc. What group?
DOCTOR (*to the patient*): What group are you? (*To the* NURSE.) Doesn't matter! I'll just get my surgical implements.
NURSE: Doesn't matter. Right.
The DOCTOR *takes his handsaw from the trolley and starts terrorising members of the audience. The* NURSE *is grabbing volunteers from the audience to give blood.*
NURSE: Sit there, you! Not squeamish, are you? Good! Can I

have two more people to hold these delicate instruments, please? Right, you stand there with this milk bottle and you take this funnel and hold the big end under his nose like that. Put the end of the tube in the milk bottle. That's it. Good. Now, it's quite painless. You won't feel a thing. Not for weeks.

DOCTOR (*meanwhile*): Right. Where's that leg? Won't take a minute. Hold still. Come off it, you big cissy. Afraid of a little bit of blood. Nurse, we've got somebody over here afraid of blood.

NURSE: Big cissy.

DOCTOR: Big cissy. Where do you think we'd be if we were afraid of a bit of blood? Get loads of it, Nurse. At least a leg full. Now anybody want her head off while I'm at it? Anybody here want his head examined? Is everything ready, Nurse?

NURSE: Nearly, Doc. I'm just explaining how painful — sorry, — painless it's going to be. I'm just going to give you a little tap on the head and all the blood'll come out of your nostrils, into the funnel, down this tube and into the milk bottle. Right? Ready? One. Two. Three.

She hits the volunteer. Blood pours into the milk bottle.

DOCTOR: Is that it? Is that all you've got?

NURSE: We need much more than that.

DOCTOR: We need a whole body full.

The volunteers are returned to their seats.

NURSE: But, Doc, where are we going to find somebody stupid enough to give us all his blood?

Enter AWFUL *being pulled by the homing device.*

AWFUL: I'm looking for the Voice. Where are you, Voice?

DOCTOR: A blood donor!

AWFUL: Eh?

NURSE: All we want is a little bit of your blood.

AWFUL: I'm sorry — I can't stop. I'm on an important mission. I'm saving the Earth.

DOCTOR: Nonsense. (*He hits him with the mallet.*) It's your civic duty to give blood.

NURSE (*taking the device*): I'll hold this for you.

It drags her round the stage. AWFUL *runs after her. The* DOCTOR *runs after* AWFUL.

NURSE: What's going on?

AWFUL: Give it back to me — I've got to get going.

DOCTOR: Come on, you big cissy — just a few pints of blood!

Enter JAKOPO *and* MARLA. *They try and fail to grab*
AWFUL. *They grab the* DOCTOR *and the* NURSE.

DOCTOR: More blood donors!

NURSE: Great!
She hits JAKOPO *and* MARLA *with the homing device and
throws it over her shoulder.* JAKOPO *and* MARLA *fall down.*
AWFUL *catches the device and goes off.*
Let's get their blood quick, Doc!
JAKOPO *and* MARLA *recover their senses.*

MARLA: Let us go, you fools! The Master shall hear of this.

DOCTOR: The master?

NURSE: Don't make me laugh! We're not frightened of *anybody!*
The VOICE *approaches.*

DOCTOR: It's him! The Voice! The master!

NURSE: The master! Let's go!
The DOCTOR *and the* NURSE *grab their things and go. The*
VOICE *arrives.*

VOICE: Bungling half-wits! Can't you do anything right?

JAK/MAR: But, master, we did our best.

VOICE: This Knawful has come too far already. I cannot go
on hiding from him. It is no longer enough that he should be
spongged. He must be destroyed. Do you understand?

JAK/MAR: Oh, yes, oh mighty one! (*They take out daggers.*) We
can kill him!

VOICE: Exactly.

JAK/MAR: Oh thank you, master, thank you.

VOICE: Just do it properly. He is heading towards the Professor's
laboratory. Follow him there and kill him. Spongg anyone
who gets in your way. Go. Go.

JAK/MAR: Yes, master. Yes, master. The master is good. The
master is good. Kill Knawful. Kill Knawful.

VOICE: Kill Knawful. Kill Knawful. Ha, ha, ha.
Exeunt JAKOPO *and* MARLA. *The* VOICE *goes.*

Scene Ten
Enter the PROFESSOR *followed by* CROTON *who wheels on a
trolley of scientific equipment.*

PROF: My friends, it is a great privilege for you to be here today.
That will do, Croton. I said leave it there. Croton!
CROTON *finally obeys.*

Prepare the playground. And, Croton, I don't want you molesting any of these children.

CROTON *prepares the playground and/or molests the audience.*

My friends, it is a great privilege for you to be here today. You are to witness the crowning triumph in the glittering career of the world's most brilliant inventor. Me. It was I who invented the perfect pet you saw earlier. It was I who invented Croton. Croton, I've warned you about that! Just ignore him if he touches you — it will wash off eventually. Croton here is the perfect servant. Efficient. Obedient. And completely devoted to his master. Aren't you, Croton?

CROTON *stares maliciously at the* PROFESSOR *who takes up a whip.*

I asked you a question, zombie! Say hello to my friends.

CROTON *makes a noise.*

And get on with your tasks, you lazy, idle, good-for-nothing, before I beat you senseless. So, you see. The perfect servant and the perfect pet. And now my latest invention is ready. It's going to be every bit as successful.

The VOICE *approaches.*

It's Voice! He must've found out about me losing the homing device by now. He'll be furious. Croton, tell him I'm not in.

He hides. CROTON *looks petrified.* VOICE *arrives.*

VOICE: Well?

CROTON: (My Master is not at home).

VOICE: Shut up, zombie. Professor, if I can see everything that happens in this kingdom what makes you think I can't see you hiding under there?

PROFESSOR *emerges holding a screwdriver.* CROTON *lurches off.*

PROF: Ah, there it is. Oh, hello, Voice!

VOICE: You blithering idiot! Your stupid homing device has brought me nothing but trouble. Knawful is pursuing me.

PROF: Sorry, Voice.

VOICE: It's no good saying sorry. You're incompetent. It's time you were sponged. None of your inventions has ever worked.

Enter CROTON *with the* ROBOT SOLDIER.

PROF: What about my robot soldiers?

VOICE: They won't work!

PROF: Of course they will.

VOICE: They won't.

PROF: I'm telling you they will.

VOICE: Show me.

PROF: Ah! .

VOICE: Now!

PROF: Tomorrow!

VOICE: Now! Or you will be spongged!

PROF (*to the* ROBOT): Please work — just once. Very well, Voice. A demonstration of my marvellous killer robots. Croton, get me two volunteers.

CROTON *gets two 'volunteers' from the audience.*

VOICE: Why does it look like that? Why are all your inventions ugly and stupid?

CROTON *insulted.*

PROF: The mechanism, Voice, is cunningly simple. Imagine that these puny weaklings were your enemies. I simply press this button and the robot is programmed to kill them. Kill!
He presses the button. The ROBOT *lurches menacingly at the victims. Just as he reaches them he grinds to a halt.*
Isn't it wonderful? Don't stop! Look, strangle the enemy! Strangle! Like this. Why do I always have to show you all what to do?
He puts his hands round one of the victims necks.
Like this. Get your hands round the neck and squeeze.
The ROBOT *puts his hands round the* PROFESSOR'S *neck.*

PROF: Very good. But squeeze much harder! Aaaaaargh! Get him off me! Croton!
*CROTON *drags the* ROBOT *off stage.* VOICE *is furious.*

VOICE: You brainless booby! You will be spongged for this. I cannot stay — the human approaches. Get the homing device back from him and you may be spared. I must go where nobody can follow — to my sanctuary in the East. Remember, Professor, get that homing device or you will be spongged.

PROF: Yes, Voice.
The VOICE *goes quickly.*
He really is becoming unbearable. I haven't got time to waste on homing devices and stupid master plans. Now where was I? Oh yes — my latest brainchild. Having already given the world the perfect pet and the perfect servant — today I reveal for the very first time my newest, most dazzling invention: The Perfect Child! Croton, bring them on.
*CROTON *brings on two evil-looking kids,* JASPER *and*

DENIS.
Aren't they beautiful? Jasper and Denis. I only finished
stitching them together today. Now all they need is a drop of
this elixir and they will have life. The perfect children. What
parent wouldn't swap one of these for *six* of you lot? Nice,
well-mannered children. Full of gaiety, but not messy. Keen
on washing dishes. Terrific at cleaning the car. Grateful for
everything; eat anything you give them. The sort of children
any parent would be proud of. This is the happiest moment of
my life.
He gives them the elixir. They come to life.
JASPER: What's on telly?
DENIS: What's that horrible smell?
JASPER: Giz somethin to eat quick.
DENIS: What's this rubbish? What you lot lookin at?
JASPER: I'm starvin. What's on telly?
DENIS: Who's this geezer with all the bandages?
JASPER: I'm *starvin!* I want somethin to eat or *else!*
DENIS: What's on telly?
JASPER: Giz some money!
PROF: Children, –
DENIS: Shut yer face!
JASPER: Got any money?
DENIS: Let's mug him!
JASPER: Yeh!
PROF: But I invented you. I gave you life!
DENIS: Let's have a fight!
JASPER: Yeh!
   JASPER *and* DENIS *start fighting.*
PROF: Stop that! You're not programmed to fight. Croton,
stop them.
   CROTON *approaches them and they stop fighting and turn on*
   him. He retreats. They start fighting again.
Stop all this I say! Look. I have presents for you.
They stop fighting.
JASPER: Presents?
DENIS: Bout time as well!
PROF: I've programmed them to be very grateful. Watch this.
He gives them a bag of sweets each.
One for you and one for you.
JASPER: What's this garbage?
DENIS: We don't want this rubbish!

They throw the sweets into the audience and turn on the
PROFESSOR.

JASP/DEN: We want *money!*

PROF: It's all right — I've programmed them to respond to firm
handling. You can't have any money! Now. I want you to
play in this playground we've designed especially for you. Go
on. Play. Be happy. .

They advance on him slowly.

JASPER: Who you talkin to?

DENIS: You lookin for trouble, furry face?

JASPER: Let's smash him!

DENIS: Yeh!

PROF: Croton. Stop them.

CROTON *shakes his head.*

Croton! I command you to stop them!

They pounce on him and beat him. Enter AWFUL. *He is
pulled round the stage by the device.*

AWFUL: Come on, Voice — where are you?

CROTON *recognises the homing device. He bashes* AWFUL
*unconscious and takes it. He waves it triumphantly and puts it
in his pocket. Meanwhile:*

PROF: All right. All right. You can have anything you want, you
monsters!

JASPER: A motorbike!

DENIS: A colour telly! One each!

PROF: Yes, yes — anything, you odious beasts!

Enter JAKOPO *and* MARLA, *daggers drawn.*

JAKOPO: We've come to kill the human!

MARLA: And we have orders to spongg anybody who gets in
our way!

JASP/DEN: Spongg! Let's go!

Exeunt JASPER, DENIS, CROTON *and the* PROFESSOR.

JAKOPO: Got him at last, Marla. How shall we destroy him?
Let's stab him.

MARLA: No. That's not painful enough. Use your imagination!

JAKOPO: Let's pull his teeth out!

MARLA: No. That's painful enough but not fatal enough. Got it!

She goes to the equipment on the trolley.

This is painful and fatal. We connect this here like this. Throw
this switch here. And the whole room will fill with deadly
nerve gas.

JAKOPO: Great!

MARLA: He'll never escape this time. When he's choked to
death we'll come back and get the homing device and return
it to the master.

JAKOPO: And can I pull his teeth out when he's dead?

MARLA: Yeh, course you can. I'll throw the switch. There. Let's
leave him to his fate. Bye, Knawful — forever!

JAKOPO: Nice knowin you, Knawful.

*They go. Gas begins to fill the room — visibly, audibly or
both. Sound of doors being locked and bolted all round as
AWFUL wakes up.*

AWFUL: What's this? It's gas! Nerve gas! I'm trapped! They've
got me this time! There's no way out! I'm a goner this time!
*He tries to find a way out but, coughing and choking, he falls
unconscious to the floor.*

INTERVAL

Scene Eleven

AWFUL *lies unconscious, spreadeagled. His hands and feet are
bound. JAKOPO and MARLA stand over him.*

MARLA: Why is he taking so long to wake up? Might have known
that nerve gas wouldn't work.

JAKOPO: Yeh — Professor Madchat invented it. Wake up,
Knawful! We want to kill you.

AWFUL *starts to wake up.*

AWFUL: No. No. Mustn't breathe gas. Got to escape. Where am
I?

JAKOPO: He's awake. Let's kill him. Quick.

MARLA: No. Slow.

JAKOPO: Yeh. Slow. Let's break every bone in his body.

MARLA: Starting with his little toes.

JAKOPO: Yeh.

AWFUL: You cowards! Why don't you untie me and fight me
properly?

The VOICE arrives.

JAK/MAR: It's the master.

VOICE: Well done, my faithful servants. You shall be rewarded.

JAK/MAR: Thank you, mighty one.

VOICE: Have you sponged him yet?

MARLA: But, master, you said we could kill him.

JAKOPO: We were going to spend all afternoon on it.

VOICE: Now that the homing device is safe again there is no
  need. It will be sufficient to spongg him. ◢
JAKOPO: But, mighty one —
VOICE: Do not argue. Where is the device? Show me it at once.
JAK/MAR: Yes, master.
  They search AWFUL.
AWFUL: Get your dirty hands off me, you creeps.
MARLA: Master — he hasn't got it.
VOICE: Imbeciles! You've done it again! You must be
  punished!
MARLA: Where is the device, Earthman?
AWFUL: Wouldn't you like to know?
VOICE: Knawful, you will save yourself a great deal of pain if
  you tell me who has the homing device. Who has it?
AWFUL: Find out!
VOICE: Spongg him!
AWFUL: No!
VOICE: We'll see how brave you are *then*. Spongg him.
JAK/MAR: Spongg him. Spongg him. Ready — spongg. Steady —
  spongg. Go! Spongg!
  AWFUL *goes rigid and makes a noise.*
VOICE: Now, Knawful. Who has that homing device?
AWFUL (*timidly*): I'm not telling you.
VOICE: Jakopo. Marla. Give him a little fright.
JAKOPO: Let's cut his tongue out — then he'll tell us.
MARLA: Yeh!
AWFUL: Aaaaaargh! No. It was the Professor's servant. That
  zombie. He took it.
VOICE: Croton — that walking first-aid kit? Jakopo. Marla.
JAK/MAR: Master?
VOICE: Find that zombie.
JAK/MAR: We obey, mighty one. What about Knawful?
VOICE: Release him. He is no threat to me any longer. He is
  now the biggest coward in the world. But I cannot rest easy
  while that homing device is out of my control. I must return
  to my sanctuary in the East where nobody can follow and
  hope to remain alive. Do not fail me again — or you will
  suffer. Go. Quickly.
  They start to go. VOICE *goes. They come back.*
MARLA: Why is master always doing us out of our fun?
JAKOPO: Let's kill him anyway.
AWFUL: No — he said you had to release me.

JAKOPO: We could make it look like an accident.

MARLA: Yeh — let's smear him with this honey and leave him
to the mercy of the killer ants.

AWFUL: No — please — no!

They smear him.

JAKOPO: He'll be eaten alive when they get a whiff of this!
Pity we can't watch — but we'll be able to hear him screaming.

AWFUL: No — please — mercy!

MARLA: Let's get that zombie, Jakopo. Bye, Knawful.

JAKOPO: See you, Knawful. We'll come back for the bones.

They go. AWFUL *writhes.*

AWFUL: No. I don't want to be eaten alive. Please — somebody
help me.

Sound of approaching ants.

What's that noise? It's the ants! They're coming for me!

Enter the KILLER ANTS.

Aaaargh. They're here. They can smell the honey. I'll just be
a skeleton when they've finished with me. It's the end. What
a way to go. I don't want to die!

The ANTS *approach. Enter the* PET.

PET: (It's my Awful!).

The PET *stamps on the* ANTS. *They run off. It unties*
AWFUL.

AWFUL: Oh, thank you! Thank you, thing! You saved my life!

PET: (What's the matter with Awful? Aaargh — he's been
spongged!).

AWFUL: It was terrible. Those two killers were horrible to me!

The PET *slaps him.*

PET: (Awful! Pull yourself together! Be brave!).

AWFUL: I can't be brave. I've been spongged. I'm a coward.
Everything's gone wrong. I'll never stop The Voice from
taking over Earth now. I've lost the homing device anyway.
Croton took it off me.

PET: (You'll just have to go and get it back).

AWFUL: I can't go and get it back. I'm too scared.

PET: (But, Awful—you're my hero!).

AWFUL: I know I'm your hero. But I'm scared.

The PET *starts to drag him off.*

PET: (Come on).

AWFUL: No. I can't.

PET: (Come on!).

AWFUL: No!

PET: (OK. You stay here and *I'll* go and get it).
AWFUL: You'll go and get it?
PET: (Yes).
AWFUL: What about me?
PET: (You stay here till I come back).
AWFUL: Stay here — on my own? But it's getting dark!
PET: (Don't be such a cissy!).
AWFUL: I'm sorry. I can't help it.
PET: (Stay here. I'm going. Goodbye).
   The PET *goes. It's getting dark.*
AWFUL: Goodbye. Come back soon. It's dark. I never used to be
   afraid of the dark. I never used to be afraid of anything till I
   got spongged.
   Enter a GIANT SPIDER *behind him.*
   Now I'm a complete coward. I don't know why I'm so scared.
   I mean, there's nothing here to harm, me is there? *(He sees it.)*
   Aaaaaaaaaargh! A giant spider! Aaaaaaaargh!
   Exit AWFUL, *pursued by* SPIDER.

Scene Twelve
Enter JAKOPO *and* MARLA.
JAK/MAR: Find Croton. Find Croton. Get the homing device.
   Get the homing device. Find Croton. Find Croton.
   Exeunt. Enter the PET, *in their tracks.*
PET: (Find Croton. Find Croton. Get the homing device. Get
   the homing device. Find Croton. Find Croton.)
   Exit PET. *Enter* JAKOPO *and* MARLA.
JAK/MAR: Find Croton. Find Croton. Get the homing device.
   Get the homing device. Find Croton Find Croton.
   Enter the PET, *in their tracks.*
PET: (Find Croton. Find Croton. Get the homing device. Get
   the —)
   JAKOPO *and* MARLA *stop, turn and face the* PET. *The* PET
   stops dead and tries to look nonchalant.
JAK/MAR: Get the Pet. Get the Pet.
PET: (Get the Pet. Get the Pet).
   Exit the PET *pursued by* JAKOPO *and* MARLA. *Enter*
   AWFUL *pursued by the* GIANT SPIDER.
AWFUL: Aaaaaaaaaaaaaaaaaaaargh!
   Exit AWFUL *pursued by* SPIDER. *Sound of galloping horses.*

Enter THE KID.

KID: Anybody here seen the Sheriff?

Enter the SHERIFF.

SHERIFF: Right behind you, Kid.

KID: Ain't gonna plug me in the back, are, you, Sheriff?

SHERIFF: Nope. I'm gonna plug you in the front.

Sponggs are visible on both COWBOYS.

KID: I'm gonna fill you full of lead, Sheriff.

SHERIFF: You're good, Kid. But everybody knows I'm the best shot in town.

They face each other, circling slowly.

KID: No you ain't. I'm the best shot in town.

SHERIFF: Oh, yeh?

KID: Yeh.

SHERIFF: Yeh?

KID: Yeh.

SHERIFF: Let's find out. Go for your gun.

KID: Ready when you are, Sheriff.

They face each other, poised to draw. Enter AWFUL, *pursued by the* SPIDER. *They cross the stage between the* COWBOYS.

AWFUL: Aaaaaaaaaaargh!

Exeunt AWFUL *and* SPIDER. *The* COWBOYS *draw and fire. They miss.*

KID: Dagnabbit!

SHERIFF: Let's do it again!

They circle each other again.

KID: You tangle with me, Sheriff, you're gonna wind up on Boot Hill.

SHERIFF: Oh yeh?

KID: Yeh.

Sound of chanting as MARLA, JAKOPO *and the* PET *draw near.*

SHERIFF: Yeh?

KID: Yeh.

SHERIFF: Let's see if you can shoot your gun as good as your mouth.

Enter the PET, *pursued by* MARLA, JAKOPO. *The* PET *passes between the* COWBOYS *who draw their guns.* JAKOPO *and* MARLA *are passing through when the* COWBOYS *shoot. They get shot to bits. Exit* PET.

SHERIFF: Dagnabbit!

KID: We just never gonna settle this since we been spongged.
SHERIFF: Same time tomorrow. I'm going home to practise.
KID: Me too!
  Exeunt the COWBOYS. JAKOPO *and* MARLA *get up
  slowly.*
JAKOPO: One day I'm going to kill everybody for this!
MARLA: Good job the master's gone to his sanctuary,
  Jakopo. He wouldn't half let us have it if he knew we'd done
  it again.
VOICE (*distant*): You cretins! Take *that!*
  They writhe in agony for a few seconds.
JAK/MAR: Mercy, master, mercy!
  The agony stops.
VOICE (*distant*): Find Professor Madchat. Wherever he is, the
  zombie will be. Wherever the zombie is, there will be the
  homing device.
JAK/MAR: Yes, master. Thank you, master. On, on, on, on, on.
  Find the Professor. Find the Professor.
  Exeunt.

Scene Thirteen
Enter the PROFESSOR *and* CROTON.
PROF: At last! I've perfected the invention I've been working on
  for the last fifty years. All my other successes pale into
  insignificance – Croton, what are you doing to those people?
  Put them down and come back here at once! All my other
  successes – the perfect pet, the perfect servant, the perfect
  child – all pale into insignificance alongside my latest creation.
  What is it that is the scourge of mankind? What is it that
  makes our lives a misery? What is it that eats all the cheese?
  YES! After fifty years of painstaking labour: my greatest
  achievement yet – The Perfect Mousetrap! Voila!
  NB. *The perfect* MOUSETRAP *can be an arrangement of
  things already onstage e.g. boxes, ropes, etc., or a new
  contraption – mechanical or human or both – which*
  CROTON *would fetch on at this point. The important things
  are that it should be laborious and inefficient and culminate
  in some kind of heavy blow.*
  Croton. The cheese, please!
  CROTON *places a piece of cheese on the floor.*

PROF: How does it work? Quite simple. As soon as your servant sees a mouse nibbling the cheese he runs to you and says "Master, a mouse is eating the cheese". Croton.
CROTON goes to him and emits some noises.
You then walk calmly to this end of the machine and insert a coin. The perfect mousetrap then springs into action.
The MOUSETRAP *lumbers into action and eventually squashes the cheese.*
Brilliant — yes? But will it work with a mouse?
CROTON shakes his head silently.
You bet it will. Watch this. Croton, a mouse, please.
CROTON produces a MOUSE *and puts it beside the cheese. The* MOUSETRAP *is set in motion. The* MOUSE *runs away before the blow is delivered.*
Of course, with some types of snivelling coward mice it is necessary to glue the mouse to the floor first. Using this Superglue — another of my inventions. Croton — another mouse, please.
CROTON glues a MOUSE *to the floor. The* MOUSETRAP *is set in motion. It misses the* MOUSE *by a mile.*
Stupid machine! Why can't you even hit a mouse when it's glued to the floor?! (*He kicks it.*) I'll give you one last chance. This time forget the mouse altogether. Put something bigger down.
CROTON sees his opportunity. He takes the homing device from his pocket and puts it beside the cheese.
Perfect. Now. Suppose that this homing device was nibbling your cheese. Croton would run to you and say "Master, a homing device is nibbling the cheese". Croton.
CROTON does it.
And you would once again insert your coin. And once again the perfect mousetrap would spring into action. Or else!
It lumbers into action.
Isn't it beautiful? Poetry to watch! I can't wait for the last bit. So satisfying! Any second now and the homing device will go pummff! (*He realises.*) Aaaaaargh! The homing device! You treacherous zombie!
He rescues the device but the MOUSETRAP *crunches his foot. Enter* JAKOPO *and* MARLA.
Aaaaaargh! My foot!
He throws the device into the air. MARLA *catches it.*
MARLA: I've got it! Master, I did it!

JAKOPO *grabs it.*

JAKOPO: No, master — *I* did it!

Enter the PET. *It grabs the device and the glue and exits.*

PET: (Geronimo!)

MARLA: You ignorant berk!

JAKOPO: Don't call me a blockhead!

MARLA: I'm going to kill you for this!

JAKOPO: Try it!

They start fighting.

PROF: You ugly, boring, mindless cretins! Get after the homing
device before Voice has me sponged! Do you hear? You'll be
boiled alive when he hears of this! Get moving!

They have turned on him.

JAK/MAR: Spongg him. Spongg him.

PROF: Now don't make me use violence on you — you'll regret
it! Croton. Protect me.

CROTON *grabs him in a vice-like grip.*

JAK/MAR: Ready — spongg. Steady — spongg. Go! Spongg!

They spongg him. It has no effect. They try again.

Ready — spongg. Steady — spongg. Go! Spongg!

Again it has no effect.

MARLA: We should've known — he's so useless already he can't
get any worse.

JAKOPO: Let's kill him then!

MARLA: Good idea.

JAKOPO: We'll kill him — then eat him alive.

MARLA: Stupid! We've no time for that. Let's just cut him into
slices.

PROF: Mercy.

They prepare to cut him up. CROTON *is delighted.*

MARLA: What's that horrible smell?

JAKOPO: It isn't me. Why do you always blame *me?*

MARLA: It's him! (*To* CROTON): Go away, you corpse!

JAKOPO: Push off, slimey. Get back to your deep freeze.

PROF: Why don't you kill *him?* He's the one who stole the device
in the first place.

JAK/MAR: Good idea.

PROF: If I may make a suggestion — unravel his bandages and
he'll fall to bits.

JAK/MAR: Yeh.

They attack CROTON. *He defeats them with brute strength.*
They run away.

PROF: Ha! You big cowards! Come back and fight me! Did you
   see the way I stood up to them? And Croton − *my* invention
   − what a success!
   CROTON *hits him over the head and carries him off.*

Scene Fourteen
Enter AWFUL, *panting.*
AWFUL: At last I've managed to get away from that spider.
   Enter the SPIDER *which chases him round the stage.*
   Aaaaaaaargh! No! Help!
   Enter the PET.
PET: (Get off my Awful!).
   The PET *and the* SPIDER *do battle. Eventually the* PET
   sprays the SPIDER *with insecticide and it goes off, coughing.*
   (Awful − are you all right?)
AWFUL: Has it gone? You saved my life again, thing. What's your
   name anyway?
PET: (Geronimo.)
AWFUL: Geronimo? You're the only friend I've got now,
   Geronimo. I'm stuck in this weird world with no way of
   getting out.
PET: (Look − the homing device).
AWFUL: You got the homing device! But it makes no difference.
   I haven't got the courage to use it anymore. I can't track the
   Voice down to his sanctuary in the East.
   The PET *hands him the device.*
PET: (Yes you can. Come on. I'll go with you).
AWFUL (*handing it back*): No. I can't.
PET (*handing it back*): (Yes you can).
AWFUL (*handing it back*): No I can't!
   The PET *coats the device with superglue and hands it back.*
PET: (Yes you can!).
AWFUL: No I − ! Hey, what's going on? It's stuck to my hand.
   Get it off. Get it off.
   The PET *activates the device. It starts dragging him.*
PET: (Awful, you've got to be brave now).
AWFUL: How can I be brave?
PET: (You must. You're my hero!).
AWFUL: I know I'm your hero but . . . . .OK. I'll try. I'll do my
   best. But will you come with me? Help me to be brave?

PET: (Yes!).

AWFUL: Let's go then. We'll track this Voice down together and try and save Earth. Awful Knawful!

PET: (Geronimo!).

    Exeunt.

Scene Fifteen

The VOICE *arrives.*

VOICE: So that coward Knawful has the device once more. The fool. He cannot hope to harm me now that he's been spongged. Even if he finds me — what can he do? All my troubles are over. It's time for me to have a little bit of fun! Ha, ha, ha, ha, ha.

    As the VOICE *goes, chaos breaks loose. Flashing lights, weird noises, wind, thunder, lightning, screams. Enter* AWFUL *and the* PET.

AWFUL: The whole place has gone crazy, Geronimo. I'm getting scared!

PET: (Come on. Keep going East!).

AWFUL: You're right. Keep going East. We're coming to find you, Voice! We're coming East.

    The horrible noises get nearer. LASSE FEVER, P.C. McKNEE, THE PROFESSOR, DOCTOR BLOOD *and the* SPIDER *all dash across stage from the east looking terrified and screaming.*

    What's going on? What's happening? What is it? I can't go on. I can't, Geronimo. What are they all so scared of? Whatever it is it was over there in the East. Let's get out of here!

PET: (No! We must go on!).

AWFUL: All right. We go on.

    They take a few more steps.

    No. It's no good. I'm too scared. Come on, Geronimo. I'm getting out of here!

    Suddenly there is silence.

VOICE: Too late, Knawful — you've arrived! Welcome. It was very considerate of you to come all this way just to bring me the homing device.

AWFUL: You'll be lucky — it's stuck to my hand for good now.

VOICE: We'll soon remedy that. Haven't you realised yet that nothing is impossible for me? We'll find a way of removing the device.

AWFUL: Come out and face me. Us.

VOICE: Not yet, Knawful, not yet. Ha, ha, ha.

AWFUL: Where are you?

The VOICE *comes from different directions.*

VOICE: Over here. Over here. Over here. Ha, ha, ha. What fun.

AWFUL: His hiding place must be near here. But where?

PET: (You go that way and I'll go that way).

AWFUL: What? OK — but don't go too far, Geronimo.

Exit the PET. AWFUL *is about to go when a* MOUTH
ORGAN *appears.*

What's this? A mouth organ.

He blows into it. It makes the sound of a church organ. Enter
A CHOIR *consisting of* DOCTOR BLOOD, McKNEE,
JAKOPO, MARLA, LASSE FEVER *and* FLORENCE *the
nurse — all in one big cassock.*

What's this? Who are you?

The CHOIR *sings.*

CHOIR: We are a friendly choir — we like to sing and play.

AWFUL: Eh? Oh, that's nice. They seem very friendly.

CHOIR (*speaking*): Yes, we are.

AWFUL: Don't I know some of you?

CHOIR (*speaking*): No. We don't think so.

AWFUL: Oh. Well — you nearly had the tune. Try it again.

CHOIR (*singing*): We are a friendly choir — we like to sing and
play. We're very glad you travelled East to play for us today.

AWFUL: Very good. Watch those high notes though.

CHOIR (*singing*): We are a friendly choir — we like to sing and
play. We're very glad you travelled East to play for us today.
We're going to chop your hand off —

Here they produce daggers, unseen by AWFUL. *He turns to
face them and they hide the daggers.*

AWFUL: No, no, no. "We're going to chop your *hand* off".
Hand. Hand. Up. Up. Try it again.

CHOIR: We are a friendly choir — we like to sing and play.
We're very glad you travelled East to play for us today.
We're going to chop your *hand* off — oh heavenly choir
rejoice!

Again the knives appear, again they hide them as AWFUL
turns.

AWFUL: Nearly, nearly. 'Rejoice'. 'Rejoice'. Up then down, see?
Are you sure I haven't seen you before?

The CHOIR *shake their heads innocently.*

AWFUL: They're the nicest people I've met since I came here. I wonder where Geronimo got to?

CHOIR (*singing*): We are a friendly choir.— we like to sing and play. We are very glad you travelled East to play for us today. We're going to chop your hand off — oh heavenly choir rejoice!

Out come the knives — they advance on AWFUL.

We're going to chop your hand off — and give it to The Voice.

AWFUL *turns and sees them.*

AWFUL: Eh? Voice? Hand? No. No. Aaaargh!

CHOIR (*singing*): Chop his hand off. Chop his hand off. Chop his hand off.

Enter the PET. *It puts itself between* AWFUL *and the daggers. The* CHOIR *is about to strike.*

VOICE: Leave them!

JAK/MAR: But, master —

VOICE: I said leave them. The Earthman has travelled far to meet me. He deserves the chance to see me once before he dies. Wait.

The homing device becomes very animated.

JAK/MAR: The Mighty One comes at last!

Except for JAKOPO *and* MARLA *the* CHOIR *run off, frightened. Enter the* MASTER. *Only his head and one arm protrude from a machine. Wires connect his head to his 'body'.*

MASTER: Welcome, Mr. Knawful. How nice to meet you.

AWFUL: You. You're the Voice. But how — ?

MASTER: A few simple gadgets.

He presses a few buttons on his machine. Lights flash. Thunder. Wind.

All very simple really. Enough to frighten my subjects — especially when they've been spongged.

AWFUL: You're just a load of wires and switches.

MASTER: Precisely. I could be rendered powerless if these wires were removed from my brain. It wouldn't take a second. If there was anyone brave enough to do it. But there isn't. Jakopo. Marla. Stand aside. I can take care of these two weaklings myself.

MARLA *and* JAKOPO *stand back.*

PET: (Go on, Awful — pull the wires out!).

AWFUL: I can't pull the wires out, Geronimo. I haven't got the guts.

MASTER: At least try, Knawful. What happened to your
  famous bravery? Ha.

  AWFUL *takes a few steps towards him but backs off again.*

AWFUL: I can't.

PET: (I'll do it).

  The PET *approaches the* MASTER.

MASTER: You stupid animal! You will die for this!
  He presses a button. A loud noise fills the air. The PET *is
  pushed violently across stage.*

AWFUL: What's happening?

MASTER: Quite simple: a moving force field. Rather effective,
  don't you think? Enough. Jakopo. Marla. Take this idiotic
  creature away and eliminate it. And have a little fun — you
  deserve it.

  They take the PET *into a corner and start to work on it.*

AWFUL: Stop it! Geronimo saved me twice. I've got to overcome
  my cowardice and save Geronimo.

MASTER (*pressing another button*): No, Knawful. I have other
  plans for you. It's time to hand over that homing device.
  Enter the ROBOT SOLDIER.

  My robot army is now ready to invade. The spongging is all
  complete. All we need now is that device. My chief robot will
  help you to remove it. Wrench his arm off!

  The ROBOT *attacks* AWFUL. *There is a big fight in which*
  AWFUL *is a victim to the* ROBOT'S *colossal strength. But
  eventually he manages to hit it over the head and send it
  haywire. It staggers off.*

MASTER: It is out of control. You have destroyed my robot.

AWFUL: Now it's your turn, you evil wretch!

MASTER: You cannot harm me, Knawful. You have no bravery.
  You have been sponged.

AWFUL: I've *got* to be brave. I've got to save Geronimo. I've
  got to destroy you and save the Earth. I've got to do it.
  He approaches the MASTER.

MASTER: Jakopo. Marla. Defend me!
  They are too busy terrorising the PET.

  You fools! Knawful, I warn you! Do not attempt to de-
  activate me. You will be electrocuted. This is not a bluff.

AWFUL: I don't believe you. Your time's up, master. Your evil
  reign's over.

MASTER: No, I'm telling the truth, Knawful. You will be

electrocuted − !
AWFUL *pulls out the wires and the* MASTER *is de-activated.*
MARLA *and* JAKOPO *stop hitting the* PET *and come into the*
centre. AWFUL *gets electrocuted. He staggers and falls lifeless.*
The PET *rushes to him.*
JAKOPO: What's happened?
MARLA: I don't feel evil anymore.
PET: (Awful. My Awful. Dead).
    Enter LASSE FEVER, DOCTOR BLOOD, FLORENCE,
    McKNEE *and* MADCHAT.
FEVER: The spongg has worn off. I can run again.
McKNEE: What's been going on here?
PET: (Awful destroyed the Master. Now he's dead. Electrocuted).
DOCTOR: Electrocuted? Run and get a blanket. Let's have a
    look at him.
    FEVER *runs off and fetches a blanket back on. The*
    PROFESSOR *is examining the remains of the* MASTER.
PROF: Brilliant! Cunningly simple! Terrific technology!
DOCTOR (*putting the blanket over* AWFUL): It's too late, I'm
    afraid. He's gone.
NURSE (*producing a milk bottle*): Won't need his blood anymore
    then, will he, Doc?
    AWFUL *throws the blanket off.*
AWFUL: Do you mind?
DOCTOR: It's a miracle!
AWFUL: I thought I was a goner that time.
PET: (My Awful!).
    In the confusion JAKOPO *and* MARLA *have been sneaking*
    off.
McKNEE: Stop, you two! You're under arrest!
    FEVER *runs and catches them.* McKNEE *handcuffs them.*
    You've got to be punished. What shall we do to them?
PET: (Tear their heads off!).
AWFUL: Don't be vindictive, Geronimo. They were in his power
    just like everybody else.
PROF: I have it! Of course − my latest invention: the perfect
    punishment. Croton.
    Enter CROTON *with three custard pies.*
    Custard pies! Get two volunteers to administer the punishment.
    AWFUL *and the* PET *get two volunteers and give them pies.*
    JAKOPO *and* MARLA *are lined up.*
    Quite simple. When I say 'go' you hit them right in the faces.

Go! Brilliant! My most successful invention yet! Absolutely − !
CROTON *hits him in the face with the third custard pie.*
Everyone sings):

AWFUL: Now the master's been destroyed it's time for me to go.
Now I've got my courage back − so it's goodbye Geronimo.
ALL: Awful Knawful saved us all − it's time to say so long.
He smashed the master into bits and beat the deadly spongg.
What an Awful man, what an Awful man, what an Awful
Knawful man!
We wish we could be Awful but we really don't think we can.
PET/CROTON: (Goodbye, Awful, goodbye. It's time to say
goodbye.

Goodbye, Awful, goodbye. We think we're going to cry).
ALL: We don't know what we're talking about but we're sure
we all agree.

Awful is our hero − he's what we'd like to be.
He's an Awful man, he's an Awful man, he's an Awful Knawful
man.

We'd all like to be Awful − but we really don't think we can.
McKNEE: If I could be like Awful I'd show a bit more gumption.
I'd round up all the villains and hit them with my truncheon.
PROF (*speaking*): My turn! Perfect verse coming up! (*Sings.*)
If I could be like Awful I'd invent a bird to fly
I'd give it wings and beaks and things and throw it in the water.
ALL: What a rotten idea, what a rotten idea, what a rotten idea,
they cried!
You couldn't be like Awful no matter how hard you tried!
Cos he's a marvellous man, he's a marvellous man, he's a
marvellous, marvellous man.
We'd all like to be marvellous, but we really don't think we can.
AWFUL *is carried out in triumph. Only the* PROFESSOR *is
left. He is fiddling with the remains of the* MASTER. *Suddenly
the* MASTER *whirs back into life. The* PROFESSOR *runs off,
scared.*
MASTER (*to the audience*): So. You. Thought. That. I. Was. De−
He blows up.

THE END

Notes on the production of
THE ADVENTURES OF AWFUL KNAWFUL

Stage Form

The play needs to move very quickly from scene to scene, with characters entering to play the next scene as the characters from the last one are making their way off. So it should be possible to stage the play successfully on any stage or in any acting area which offers more than one entrance. Proscenium arch staging might prove more difficult than other forms because the play clearly benefits from giving such characters as Croton, Jakopo, Marla, Doctor Blood and Florence easy access to the audience.

Scene One

The pre-play action on the adventure playground depends of course on what is onstage. If the scenic props have been kept to a minimum, or if it is not thought prudent to have the audience invading the acting area, then it is possible to begin with the entry of the Playleader followed immediately by the noise of the helicopter and the entry of Sid and the bodyguards. The first few lines can then be modified. Instead of telling the audience to sit down Sid might order them to turn out their pockets while the bodyguards search for offensive weapons.

It will be clear in this scene which of the props referred to in the script are essential and which are only preferable. The bicycle, for instance, is essential; the microphone is a good idea if possible.

If the play is being presented in a limited space with no suitable exit, Awful should simply get as long an approach as possible onstage before riding his bike into the stunt.

Scene Two

Jakopo and Marla could either have their legs strapped together — as in a three-legged race — or be joined by a length of rope or material. The latter makes them more manoeuvrable.

It is essential that The Voice be amplified and that the actor/actress who plays The Voice should remain unseen until the end of the play.

Scene Nine

If it is not possible to have a door for Doctor Blood he can battle his way onto the stage into the wind (an essential sound effect, this) and fall over when it stops.

Florence (who should be played by a man) need not have a trolley. A tray, even a carrier bag, would do.

The blood donation: The length of tubing contains coloured liquid and is stopped at the milk-bottle-end. Provided this end of the tube is unplugged at the right moment (i.e. during the briefing of the 'volunteer', when it is then inserted into the milk bottle) and provided that the milk-bottle is not lowered to a level below that of the funnel-end of the tube until the right moment (i.e. at the blow of the mallet) then the 'blood' should flow into the milk-bottle. Otherwise, if the trick proves too difficult to stage, have no blood in the tube but play the lines anyway as they are written.

Scene Ten

The Robot Soldier should be completely inactive until the Professor presses its buttons. If possible have Croton carry it on. Jasper and Denis should be played by adults.

If no blackout is available for the end of the scene, Awful should crawl/stagger off and be brought on and bound, still unconscious, after the interval.

Scene Eleven

In the RSC production the army of killer ants consisted of a row of buttons on a thread which was pulled across the floor of the stage by unseen hands in the wings. Another way of doing this might be to have costumed actors — like the Giant Spider, who was played by an actor in a boiler suit with extra arms and legs sown on.

Scene Fifteen

In the RSC production the Voice's contraption was based on a wheelchair. A box was built over this and it had knobs, switches and wires on it.

Peter Flannery

Musical Notes

The first thing to say about *The Adventures of Awful Knawful* is that it is not a musical and that I see no reason why the play could not be successfully staged without any music whatsoever.

Having said that, I would like to encourage anyone contemplating doing a production, to use as much music as possible by drawing on whatever musical talents and resources are available to them. *Awful Knawful* is a play packed with a terrific amount of action and in the production at the RSC we found a great deal of fun and tension was gained by accompanying the action sequences with music. The original score for the music is printed in this playtext and you are welcome to adapt it, follow it, ignore it or just to use it as a starting point for your own score. The important thing is to see what musical talents and instruments you have available and start from there. You might consider having a band separate from the actors or you could use the actors themselves to create the music. Expert musicians are a bonus, not a necessity. After all, the main part of the play takes place in the abnormal world of failures and incompetents, and I see no reason why the band should be excluded from the Voice's master plan. In the RSC production we had a separate band because the musicians were available and that band consisted of: Percussion, Bassoon, Horn, Trumpet and Flute. But a band made up of Percussion, Kazoos and Voices would have worked just as well. I have made some notes about specific cues which might be of some help when looking at the score and seeing how the music fits in.

One final point, the style of the music is heavily based on comic horror movies and the rhythms to the soundtrack of *Jaws*. Discords are most welcome!

1. **Fanfare for Awful and Awful's March**
   It might be an idea to use recorded music here so that a difference is noticed in the music when Awful crashes into the world ruled by the Voice.

2. **Effect for Entrance and Exit of Voice**
   A long crescendoing bass note was used with a bell to cut off the effect just before the Voice speaks. When the Voice goes, the bell sounded first and then the bass note faded away. It is very useful to have a fairly long musical cue, since the audience and characters all know the Voice is coming and this can add to tension.

3. **Music for Actual Spongging**
   The 4th and final bar shows a downward chromatic run and this should have the effect of sounding as if the band is laughing at the victims. The cue should be repeated everytime someone is spongged.

4. **Music for the Chase of the Athlete**
   This music should begin as soon as the Athlete runs from the hands of Jakopo and Marla. It ceases when he leaves the stage and begins whenever he reappears running. It ends forever once he has been spongged.

5. **Croton's Theme**
   Another recurring theme which accompanies the character whenever suitable.

6. **Minefield Music**
   The length of this piece is obviously determined by the obstacles confronting Awful in his crossing of the minefield. If you find the cue needs lengthening I suggest you repeat the first bar at a slow pace and with a pause between each repeat, then launch into the piece and repeat the last but one 3/4 bar until Awful has reached the other side of the minefield, then proceed with fanfare.

7. **The Homing Device**
   A Swannee whistle is very effective for this when the device starts working.

8. **Music for Pursuing Spider**
   First three bars should play over Awful's lines: 'Now I'm a complete coward. . . .etc.'. As soon as Awful screams at seeing the Spider the frantic section at bar 4 should begin. The music from bar 4 is repeated everytime Awful is pursued by Spider and also when Geronimo frightens the Spider away.

9. **Music for the perfect Mousetrap**
   Accompanies the Mousetrap while in motion. The music stops dead when the weight drops onto the ground at the end of the Mousetrap's manoeuvres. The Swannee whistle accompanying the dropping of the final weight is very useful. Music restarts with Mousetrap.

10. **Awful Requiem Music**
    To be played whilst Awful is unconscious, presumed dead by electrocution.

11. **Awful Song**
    Only the first verse of lyrics has been printed, but the rest are

easily fitted in. The final reprise of 'He's a marvellous man' is a repeat of the chorus tune.

12. **Percussion**

There is no limit to the amount of percussion used and the greater the variety of sounds the better. Percussion can be used to highlight Jakopo and Marla, the Robot, the Ants etc.

13. **The Choir**

This can be sung unaccompanied. The lyrics can also be sung to the tune of *The Holly and the Ivy*.

Mick Ford

Music for the Play

1

AWFUL MARCH 2

FANFARE FOR SPONGGING CEREMONY 3

♪ = 144
raucous

MUSIC FOR THE ACTUAL SPONGG 4

♩ = 96

Jakopo & Maela.

CROTON'S THEME (SLOW, CREEPY, WITH THE OCCASIONAL LOUD CHORDAL SURPRISE) 6

* The Eb passing notes at the beginning of bars 2 & 4 are isolated Eb's. All other E's in said bars are ♮.

Music to highlight the revelation of the Coppers Spongg

♩ = 60

with attack

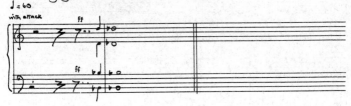

MINEFIELD MUSIC — TO ACCOMPANY AWFUL AS HE CROSSES MINEFIELD ⑺

♩ = 180

incessant / lively

GAS MUSIC LEADING TO INTERVAL [8]

MARCH OF THE KILLER ANTS 9

Music for Pursuing Spider (1st 3 bars are only played on Spider's 1st entrance begin bar 4 immediately when Awful screams) 10

(SLOW SPOOKY) p

(frantic) ff

SEDATELY.

REPEAT FROM A

CHOIR: WE ARE A FRIENDLY CHOIR [12]

♩ = 100

like a carol

WE ARE A FRIEND-LY— CHOIR— WE
C   F

LIKE TO SING AND PLAY— WE'RE VE-RY GLAD YOU
B♭   F   Dm   B♭

tra—velled East to— play for us to— day— we're
C   F   C   G   C

go-ing to chop your hand off Oh! Hea-ven-ly choir re—
A   Dm.   F

-Joice— we're go-ing to- chop your hand off and
C   B♭   C

give it to The voice—
B♭   C   F

CHOIR: "CHOP YOUR HAND OFF CHANT" [13]

CHOP HIS HAND OFF   CHOP HIS HAND OFF   CHOP HIS HAND OFF   CHOP HIS HAND OFF
Fm   Dm   Fm   Dm

Robot FIGHT MUSIC 14

♪ = 180
fast

repeat from A

CONT. OVER
PAGE.

MOURNFUL
SLOW ♩ = 60

AWFUL SONG [16]

lively ♩ = 144.

(AWFUL) 1. Now The Mas-ters been de—stroyed it's
(ALL)   Aw - ful know-ful saved us all   it's

time for me to go—— Oh now I've got my cou-rage back so it's good—
time to say so long—— he smashed the mas-ter in - to bits— and

C A Dm. G C

D G